LEONARDO'S "QUOTEBOOK"

Thoughts By and About
Leonardo da Vinci

SELECTIONS CHOSEN AND COMMENTS EDITED BY
GODFREY HARRIS

THE AMERICAS GROUP

The Americas Group
9200 Sunset Blvd., Suite 404
Los Angeles, California 90069-3506
U.S.A.
☎ + (1) 310 278 8038
FX + (1) 310 271 3649
EM hrmg@aol.com
www.AmericasGroup.com

ISBN:
978-0-935047-57-8

Library of Congress Cataloging-in-Publication Data

Leonardo, da Vinci, 1452-1519.
Leonardo's "quotebook" : thoughts by and about Leonardo da Vinci
/ comments and selections edited by Godfrey Harris. -- 1st ed.
p. cm.
Includes bibliographical references and index.
ISBN-13: 978-0-935047-57-8 (alk. paper)
1. Leonardo, da Vinci, 1452-1519--Quotations. 2. Leonardo, da
Vinci, 1452-1519--Juvenile literature.   I. Harris, Godfrey, 1937-   .
II. Title.
N6923.L33A35 2007
709.2--dc22

2006021658

Printed in India
Aegean Offset Printing

TABLE OF CONTENTS

OTHER BOOKS BY GODFREY HARRIS

What a Great Idea!
The Definitive Southern California Diet (with Jeffrey I. Barke, M.D.)
The Hottest Ideas in Word of Mouth Advertising
The Complete Business Guide
The Essential Gift Planning Kit
The Essential Diet Planning Kit (with Jeffrey I. Barke, M.D.)
The Essential Wedding Planning Kit
The Essential Cooking Planning Kit
The Essential Project Planning Kit
Civility
Corruption
The Essential Moving Planning Kit—1st, 2nd, & 3rd Editions (with Mike H. Sarbakhsh)
The Essential Travel Planning Kit—1st & 2nd Editions
Grandparenting
The Essential Event Planning Kit—1st, 2nd, 3rd, 4th, 5th, 6th, & 7th Editions
Watch It!
Concentration—1st & 2nd Editions (with Kennith L Harris)
Let Your Fingers Do the Talking
Talk Is Easy
The Ultimate Black Book—3rd Edition (with Kennith L Harris and Mark B Harris)
Don't Take Our Word for It!
How to Generate Word of Mouth Advertising (with Gregrey J Harris)
Promoting International Tourism—1st & 2nd Editions (with Kenneth M. Katz)
European Union Almanac—1st & 2nd Editions (with Hans J. Groll and
   Adelheid Hasenknopf)
The Panamanian Problem (with Guillermo de St. Malo A.)
Mapping Russia and Its Neighbors (with Sergei A. Diakonov)
Power Buying (with Gregrey J Harris)
Talk Is Cheap (with Gregrey J Harris)
The Fascination of Ivory
Invasion (with David S. Behar)
The Ultimate Black Book—2nd Edition (with Kennith L Harris)
The Ultimate Black Book—1st Edition
The Panamanian Perspective
Commercial Translations (with Charles Sonabend)
From Trash to Treasure (with Barbara DeKovner-Mayer)
Panama's Position
The Quest for Foreign Affairs Officers (with Francis Fielder)
The History of Sandy Hook, New Jersey
Outline of Social Sciences
Outline of Western Civilization

INTRODUCTION

Leonardo da Vinci lived more than 500 years ago and produced some of the world's most important paintings. He was also an an architect, designer, engineer, and scientist. He learned to use art, anatomy, botany, geology, mathematics, and physics to build on what was known in his day and to improve on his own concepts.

Because he was generating so many new ideas and improving on what had been developed by others, he inevitably drew sketches and took notes on his ideas and what he observed around him. The images and thoughts were captured in numerous sketchbooks—amounting to more than 14,000 pages. After Leonardo's death in 1519, Fancisco Melzi, his assistant, carefully cataloged and preserved these notebooks. But after Melzi died, the sketchbooks were cut apart and their individual elements disbursed. They were subsequently brought back in multiple new volumes known as codices—sometimes in an organized fashion, sometimes in a jumble of unconnected subjects.

Modern scholars have given these known Codices names with slight variations to accommodate for English, French,

Spanish and Italian useage. This book has adopted the following names for its references:

- Codice Atantico
- Codice Trivulznius
- Codice Marciano
- Codice on Birds
- Codice Arundel
- Codice Foster
- Windsor Collection
- Manuscripts Madrid
- Paris Manuscripts
- Codice Leicester

They are located in various respositories in Europe and the United States. The first two — Atlantico and Trivulznius — are in Milan; Marciano is in Venice. Codices Arundel, Foster and Windsor are in the United Kingdom. Codice Leicester is in Seattle, Washington, the property of Bill Gates, the Chairman of Microsoft. Individual Da Vinci sketches that were never put back into one of the codices are known to be in both private hands as well as museum collections.

All the quotations attributed to Leonardo da Vinci are drawn from secondary sources translated from the 15th century Tuscan dialect by unknown individuals. As a result, we have clarified some where their rendering into English was not clear. Our hope is that we have captured Leonardo's most important and relevant thoughts for the modern world and that we have also illuminated his fascinating personality a little better with the quotations we have included from others.

Los Angeles, Ca.   Godfrey Harris
August 2006

UNDERSTANDING LEONARDO DA VINCI

Leonardo da Vinci is one of the most intriguing men in history—an ordinary man who did extraordinary things. How did this one individual come to accomplish so many things in so many fields? Why this man at this time in human history?

No one, of course, is quite sure, but Leonardo's overwhelming desire to succeed seems to have been driven by forces greater than his insatiable curiosity and enormous imagination. One theory holds that his childhood was filled with such personal doubts and family uncertainties that he did everything in his power throughout his life to ensure that he was not forgotten or ignored, that his work and effort would receive the respect and attention he sought and thought he deserved.

As a child born out of wedlock, Leonardo would be denied the right to enter a profession, obtain a place at the university, or gain social access to the royal courts. On top of this, Leonardo was determinedly left-handed in an era when people were taught that such activity was literally sinister—a tool of the devil—and something to be avoided. Leonardo dealt with this by perversely writing from right to left, and backwards. Was this to avoid smudging the writing or to keep prying eyes from readily reading his ideas as some believe? Or was it merely Leonardo's way to draw attention to his ideas, his sketches—and himself? And if these two factors were not enough to cope with, Leonardo had to confront a third factor in the years to come: He was almost certainly homosexual at a time when such behavior was subject to severe penalties and public ostracism.

Given his status and prospects in society, his father hoped that the boy's great interest and obvious talent for drawing might qualify him for an apprenticeship. It did. Popular artisan Andrea del Verrocchio headed one of Florence's leading craft studios—where everything from furniture to religious objects, from paintings to statues—were crafted for the city's aristocracy and wealthy merchants. His apprenticeship to one of Florence's leading artists would give him the training and experience that could serve him well in the future—as well as help him rise above the circumstances of his birth.

Leonardo served as Verrocchio's assistant for nearly 9 years and during this time learned a dozen different crafts. He was famously given the honor of providing an angel in the corner of a painting that became known as the *Baptism of Christ*. Legend has it that Leonardo's contribution to that painting was so extraordinary in execution that Verrocchio himself pledged never to paint anything else ever again.

In the atmosphere of Veracchio's all-male studio, his left handedness may well have been embraced for the authority it gave his brush strokes and his homosexual tendencies may well have been welcomed. Because of his acceptance in the studio and its relative safety from the harsher attitudes of the outside world, Leonardo did not hesitate to take great risks in his work and his thinking. It was these intellectual, artistic, and personal risks that may well have provided the stimulus for the great advances that he would later make and that we marvel at today.

For example, in the field of art he was one of the first to experiment with oil-based paints because of their flexibility and luminosity. Leonardo quickly mastered the crucial skill of perspective to create detailed background scenes and he experimented with blending light and dark areas seamlessly to give his paintings a more realistic look. He invented a surface for frescos that permitted him to work at his own speed rather than at a pace that the traditional methods required.

In his desire for attention and recognition, he also showed an unbridled willingness to do whatever was asked of him to gain the approval of his patrons and their friends. We never think of him as such, but in modern terms his desire to please helped Leonardo to become a superb event planner, a skilled costume designer, a brilliant lighting technician, a resourceful impresario, and an accomplished musician. A number of the machines that Leonardo developed were not for some practical engineering purpose, but simply to entertain and dazzle the royal guests at various social functions.

When Milan was faced with the threat of invasion by the French in the late 1490s, he volunteered to develop machines and engineering strategies to assist Duke Ludavico Sforza in repelling the foe. Many of the machines Da Vinci sketched and described—for war or for engineering purposes—were probably never built because they required too much money, too many scarce materials, or too many experiments to perfect their use or performance. But many of these projects embodied ideas and concepts we know and enjoy today, such as:

- The transfer of energy through a chain.

- The repetitive accuracy of a cam hammer.

- The safety features of a worm screw.

- The weight-bearing capacity of a central crane

- The equalizing role of a differential gear

- The capability of a water-powered saw

  and drill.

Perhaps because of his insatiable curiosity, perhaps because he could never seem to harness his mind to concentrate on one topic until he completely mastered it, perhaps because of his overpowering need to achieve perfection, he kept seeing ways to improve on the performance of objects then in common use.

- The use of multiple pulleys
  to lift weighty items with
  the same motive force,
  but at the sacrifice of speed.

- The use of a candle of a
  specific diameter and a
  chart precisely carved into
  a backdrop to calculate the
  passage of time as the
  candle melted on dark nights.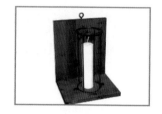

The patience and persistence he exhibited to accurately tell time at night revealed a pattern that would mark all of Leonardo's efforts as a designer and engineer: if it wasn't perfect it wasn't finished. Because of this he rarely saw projects to completion. In fact, a younger Michelangelo criticized Da Vinci for his procrastination. Was this seeming indolence triggered by his perfectionism or by his constant inquisitiveness? Anything that he observed in nature could trigger a flood of questions in his mind about how it functioned, how it accomplished particular tasks, and the purpose each of its attributes served. None more so than his fascination with birds to unlock the secrets of flight.

His desire to be free from the confines of earth suggests the confidence he had that there was nothing he couldn't accomplish if he put his mind to finding a solution. Evidence of that confidence and his desire for perfection can be found in his constant sketching and voluminous notes to portray his subjects and operate devices as accurately and as efficiently as possible.

For Leonardo, nature was the perfect machine that had to be understood completely in order to be emulated as closely as possible in man-made efforts. That is why he became skilled as an anatomist—to learn how the muscles, tendons, and skeletal structure worked together to make a smile or raise an arm, why he theorized on how the fossils he found high in the Alps might have gotten there, and why the few paintings he attempted—only some 14 are known to have survived to the modern era—were renowned then as now for the subtly, accuracy, and secrets they embodied.

The best way to form your own impression of this remarkable man and what he accomplished is to remember what he once proclaimed...

The natural desire of good men is knowledge.

and to contemplate what others have said about him. This, in the words of author E. L. Kongsburg:

*[Leonardo] could not look at things made by God
without wondering how He had made them,
and he could not look at things made by man
without thinking of some way to make them better.*

TIMELINE

YEAR	LEONARDO'S LIFE	ELSEWHERE
1452	Born out-of-wedlock near Vinci in Tuscany in April. Barred from taking his father's name, he becomes Leonardo "of Vinci."	
1453		Constantinople and the Byzantine Empire fall to the Turks, and many intellectuals and their scholarly manuscripts find their way to Italy.
1458		Guttenberg introduces moveable type for a printing press.
1467	Begins a 12-year apprenticeship in Andrea del Verrocchio's Florence studio.	
1472	Accepted into Guild of Florentine Painters and completes *The Annunciation*—his first major painting.	
1475	Ser Piero, Leonardo's father, has a legitimate son by his third wife, ending Leonardo's hope for any inheritance.	
		The rifle is invented.
1476	Contributes angel to Verrocchio's *Baptism of Christ*. Accused of sodomy, but the charges were later dropped for lack of evidence.	
		Inca Empire takes control of South America from Ecuador to Argentina.
1477		The Netherlands,

YEAR	LEONARDO'S LIFE	ELSEWHERE
		Luxembourg, and Burgundy join the Holy Roman Empire, based in Vienna.
1478	Leonardo receives first commission as an independent artist at the age of 26. Paints the portrait of *Ginevra de' Benci*.	
1481		Mongols defeated and driven from Russia.
1482	Leaves Lorenzo d'Medici's Florence for Milan and becomes an employee of Duke Ludivico (il Moro) Sforza, where Leonardo plays the lyre and remains some 18 years as an artist, event planner, and engineer in residence. Most of Leonardo's labor-saving machines and mechanical devices are designed during this period of his life.	
1484	Begins his serious study of flight. He builds flying machines until 1489.	
		The plague sweeps Europe, killing huge numbers.
1485	Paints *Lady with an Ermine*, a portrait of Cecilia Gallerine, thought to be the Duke's mistress. Begins painting *Virgin of the Rocks*.	
		Bartolomeu Dias sails around the Cape of Good Hope for Portugal.
		The Wars of the Roses

YEAR	LEONARDO'S LIFE	ELSEWHERE
		between two houses of the English throne ends.
1487	Begins his daring study of anatomy with his first autopsies.	
1489	Draws the *Vitruvian Man* exploring harmonious proportions.	
1492	Becomes military engineer to Cesare Borgia, Duke of Florence, and Pope Alexander VI's son. Borgia is the model for Niccolò Machiavelli's *The Prince*.	
1492		Columbus reaches the New World.
1493	Builds clay model for huge bronze horse as tribute to Duke Francisco Sforza, Ludovico's father; it is unveiled at the wedding celebration of Sforza's neice.	
1495	Leonardo begins work on *The Last Supper* in a Milanese monastery; finishes this work in 1497.	
1496	Ready for his first flight.	
1498		The Fench capture Milan.
1499	French soldiers use the clay horse for target practice after Sforza's palace is captured.	
	Leonardo presents his ideas for underwater defenses to the	

	Duke of Venice to protect against a Turkish naval invasion. The ideas are rejected.	
		Vasco da Gama opens route to India around Africa.
1500	Rivalry with Michelangelo becomes public.	Half-millenium recognized and celebrated by the Catholic Church.
1502		The first portable clock is invented.
1503	Begins the *Mona Lisa,* works on it for the rest of his life. Commissioned to paint *Battle of Anghiari.*	
1504	Leonardo meets Michelangelo; later in the year Leonardo's father dies.	
		The Holly Roman Em peror honors the memory of the Dutch fisherman who started pickling her- ring in brine—an impor- tant method of preserving food at the time.
1507	Francesco Melzi, Leonardo's faith- ful assistant, begins work. Leonardo describes the effects of arterial sclerosis for the first time.	
		King Henry VIII's reign in England begins.

YEAR	LEONARDO'S LIFE	ELSEWHERE
1509	Leonardo draws detailed maps and conducts his geological studies.	
1510		Coffee, as a social drink, reaches Mecca and Cairo from its origins in Yemen.
1512		Michelangelo completes painting the ceiling of the Sistine Chapel at the Vatican.
1513	Leonardo returns to Rome.	
1515	Leonardo's mechanical lion is presented to the King of France as a gift from the Duke of Urbino.	
1516	Moves to Chateau Amboise in France to work for King Francis I until his death.	
1517	Leonardo suffers a stroke paralyzing his *right* side.	Martin Luther calls for reform of the Catholic Church.
1519	Leonardo dies on May 2 in France.	
		Cortez arrives in Mexico.

Leonardo da Vinci

In Leonardo's Words

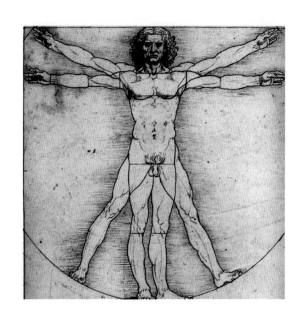

ON LIFE

The natural desire of good men is knowledge.

*The eye is
the window
of the soul.*

Wisdom is the daughter of experience.

*Every
difficulty
can be
overcome
by
effort.*

... acquire diligence rather than rapidity.

It is easier to resist at the beginning than at the end.

Obstacles cannot crush me.
Every obstacle yields
to stern resolve.

*You do ill if you praise,
but worse if you censure
what you do not
understand.*

Necessity is the mistress and guide of nature.

*Patience serves as
a protection against wrongs
as clothes do against cold.
For if you put on more clothes
as the cold increases,
it will have no power
to hurt you.
So in like manner
you must grow in patience
when you meet with
great wrongs, and
they will then be powerless
to vex your mind.*

*We know very well that errors
are better recognized in the
works of others
than in our own;
and that often, while reproving
little faults in others,
you may ignore
great ones in yourself.*

Iron rusts from disuse;
water loses its purity
from stagnation and
in cold weather [it]
becomes frozen;
[in the same way] …
inaction saps
the vigors of the mind.

Every now and then go away,
have a little relaxation,
for when you
come back to work,
your judgment will be surer.
... to remain constantly
at work will cause you
to lose power of judgment.

*... tears
come from the heart
and not from the
brain.*

Intellectual passion
dries out
sensuality.

As a well-spent day brings happy sleep, so a life well used brings happy death.

*If you are alone,
you belong entirely
to yourself. If you are
accompanied by even one
companion, you belong
only to half yourself,
or even less.*

*[God] creates
nothing
superfluous
or
imperfect.*

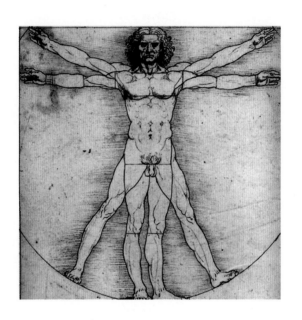

ON EDUCATION

*Whoever in discussion
adduces authority
uses not intellect
but memory.*

*...my opinion
was based upon
observation;
... to be learned in books means
only to have
an opinion on
other people's opinons.*

Study without desire spoils the memory, and it retains nothing that it takes in.

Festival is like lightning.
It has no history, and
it has no future.
It lights up everything
for a brief second.
It passes.
It leaves nothing of itself
save its effect.

He who is fixed
to a star
does not
change his mind.

ON HEALTH

*To keep in health,
this rule is wise:
Eat only when you want and
relish food.
Chew thoroughly that
it may do you good.
Have it well cooked,
unspiced and undisguised.**

---

* Leonardo became a vegetarian at some point in his life.

*Pleasure and Pain
[are] twins,
since there never is one
without the other.*

*The incessant current
of the blood
through the veins
makes these veins thicken
and become callous,
so that at last they close up
and prevent the
passage of blood**

* With this observation, Leonardo identified how cholesterol works to deposit plaque along the walls of the arteries.

*Movement
will fail
sooner
than
usefulness.*

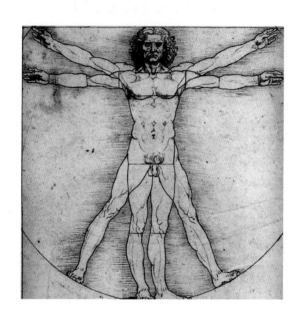

ON NATURE

*Nature
never breaks
her own
laws.*

*Water
is the
driving force
of
nature.*

...human ingenuity...
will never devise any
inventions more beautiful,
nor more simple,
nor more to the purpose than
Nature does.

*When you draw
from nature
stand at a distance of
three times the height
of the object
you wish to draw.*

The walking of man is always after the universal manner of walking in animals with four legs ... crosswise; that is, if he puts forward his right foot in walking he puts forward with it, his left arm and vice versa.

When once you have
tasted flight,
you will forever
walk the earth
with your eyes
turned skyward,
for there you have been,
and there you will always
long to return.

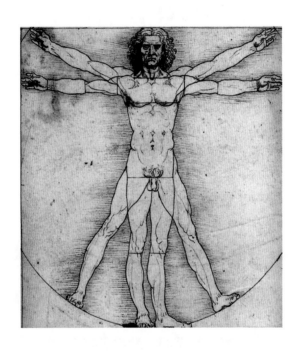

ON SCIENCE

*Those who become
enamored of practices
without science
are like sailors
who go aboard ship without
a rudder and compass,
for they are never certain
where they will land.*

The book
of the science of
mechanics
must precede
the book of
useful
inventions.

*Experience
does not ever err.
It is only your judgment
that errs in promising itself
results which are not caused
by your experiments.*

*The arch is nothing else
than a force originated
by two weaknesses,
for the arch ... is composed of
two segments of a circle,
each of which being very weak
... tends to fall;
but as each opposes this
tendency in the other,
the two weaknesses combine
to form one strength.*

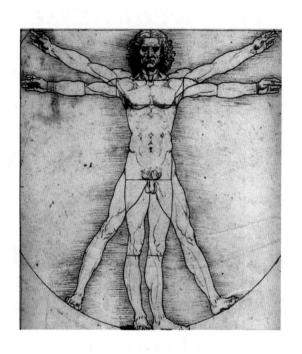

ON ART

The poet ranks far below the painter in the representation of visible things, and far below the musician in that of invisible things.

*What is fair
in men passes away,
but not so in art.*

… take a note …
in a little book
which you should always
carry with you [and]
preserve with great care;
for the forms, and positions
of objects, are so infinite
that the memory is incapable
of retaining them,
wherefore keep these sketches
as your guides and masters.

The mind of the painter
must resemble a mirror,
which always takes
the color of the object
it reflects
and is completely occupied
by the images
of as many objects
as are in front of it.

*Of several bodies,
all equally large and
equally distant,
that which is most
brightly illuminated
will appear to the eye
nearest and largest.**

---

* Leonardo's use of light in his paintings are among his most important contributions.

Every object we see
will appear larger at midnight
than at midday, and
larger in the morning
than at midday.
This happens because
the pupil of the eye
is much smaller at midday
than at any other time.

He is a
poor disciple
who does
not excel
his
master.

Leonardo da Vinci

In the Words of Others

Leonardo da Vinci was
like a man
who awoke too early
in the darkness,
while the others
were all still asleep.

Sigmund Freud

[Leonardo] could not look at things made by God without wondering how He had made them, and he could not look at things made by man without thinking of some way to make them better.

E. L. Kongsburg
The Second Mrs. Gionconda

[Leonardo da Vinci]
turned the
flow of science
into a
tempestuous torrent.

Duhem

... Leonardo never chose
to work fast.
Time was his enemy,
and he never wanted
to be at its mercy.

E. L. Kongsburg
The Second Mrs. Gioncondo

Leonardo as a young man [had] personal beauty [that] could not be exaggerated, whose every movement was grace itself and whose abilities were so extraordinary that he could readily solve every difficulty…[with] a spirit and courage invariably royal and magnanimous….and could sing and improvise divinely...

Giorgio Vasari*

* Vasari was an artist himself, but he is perhaps better known as the first art historian.

[Leonardo]
was not only a great painter
but also a great
mathematician, mechanic
and engineer, to whom the
most diverse branches of
physics are indebted for
important discoveries.*

Frederick Engels

---

* Although Engels did not specify any particular advance, certainly Leonardo's discovery that air has many of the characteristics of water is among his most important contributions to the field of physics.

The great mound of talent
and intellect called
Leonardo da Vinci
has a very thin skin.
Very thin.
He deflates at the
tiniest prick.

E. L. Kongsburg
The Second Mrs. Gionconda

Historians still debated
whether Da Vinci wrote
[in mirrored script]
simply to amuse himself
or to keep people from …
stealing his ideas, but the
point was moot.
Da Vinci did as he pleased.

Dan Brown
The Da Vinci Code

He was never comfortable
when people and emotions
got too close;
a human situation could
show him to be
less than perfect.

E. L. Kongsburg
The Second Mrs. Gionconda

Leonardo da Vinci, Michelangelo, and Raphael are the Book of the World.

Benvenuto Cellini

In Italy for thirty years
under the Borgias
they had warfare, terror,
murder and bloodshed
but they produced
Michelangelo,
Leonardo da Vinci and
the Renaissance.
In Switzerland,
they had brotherly love;
they had five hundred years
of democracy and peace and
what did that produce?
The cuckoo clock.

Orson Wells
"The Third Man"

He labored
much more
by his word
than in fact
or by deed.

Giorgio Vasari

Maybe Da Vinci's plethora of tantalizing clues [about the whereabouts of the Holy Grail) was nothing but an empty promise left behind to frustrate the curious and bring a smirk to the face of his knowing Mona Lisa.

Dan Brown
The Da Vinci Code

[Francis I of France]
did not believe that
any other man
had come into the world
who had attained so great
a knowledge as Leonardo,
and that not only
as sculptor, painter, and
architect,
for beyond that
he was a
profound philosopher.

Benvenuto Cellini

Index

GODFREY HARRIS has been a public policy consultant based in Los Angeles, California, since 1968. He began consulting after serving as a university lecturer, U.S. Army intelligence officer, U.S. foreign service officer with the Department of State, an organizational specialist in President Lyndon Johnson's Executive Office, and as a program manager for an international financial company in Geneva. As President of Harris/Ragan Management Group, Harris has focused the firm's activities on projects that offer alternative solutions to matters of community concern.

Given the number and variety of projects he has been involved with over his 40-year career, it was not unusual for him to accept the challenge of finding suitable venues in the northeastern portion of the Pacific Rim for an exhibit of the machines designed and described by Leonardo da Vinci. It was in the course of assuming the role of curator of the exhibit that Harris began his study of Leonardo. It is from his readings that the quotations in this book arise.

This is the 54th book he has written on his own or with associates. He holds degrees from Stanford University and the University of California, Los Angeles.

The Life and Contributions of Leonardo da Vinci (with Thomas Mankowski)
Coloring with Leonardo (with Daniel Mankowski)
What a Great Idea!
The Definitive Southern California Diet (with Jeffrey I. Barke, M.D.)
The Hottest Ideas in Word of Mouth Advertising
The Complete Business Guide
The Essential Gift Planning Kit
The Essential Diet Planning Kit (with Jeffrey I. Barke, M.D.)
The Essential Wedding Planning Kit
The Essential Cooking Planning Kit
The Essential Project Planning Kit
Civility
Corruption
The Essential Moving Planning Kit—1st, 2nd, & 3rd Editions (with Mike H. Sarbakhsh)
The Essential Travel Planning Kit—1st & 2nd Editions
Grandparenting
The Essential Event Planning Kit—1st, 2nd, 3rd, 4th, 5th, 6th, & 7th Editions
Watch It!
Concentration—1st & 2nd Editions (with Kennith L Harris)
Let Your Fingers Do the Talking
Talk Is Easy
The Ultimate Black Book—3rd Edition (with Kennith L Harris and Mark B Harris)
Don't Take Our Word for It!
How to Generate Word of Mouth Advertising (with Gregrey J Harris)
Promoting International Tourism—1st & 2nd Editions (with Kenneth M. Katz)
European Union Almanac—1st & 2nd Editions (with Hans J. Groll and Adelheid Hasenknopf)
The Panamanian Problem (with Guillermo de St. Malo A.)
Mapping Russia and Its Neighbors (with Sergei A. Diakonov)
Power Buying (with Gregrey J Harris)
Talk Is Cheap (with Gregrey J Harris)
The Fascination of Ivory
Invasion (with David S. Behar)
The Ultimate Black Book—2nd Edition (with Kennith L Harris)
The Ultimate Black Book—1st Edition
The Panamanian Perspective
Commercial Translations (with Charles Sonabend)
From Trash to Treasure (with Barbara DeKovner-Mayer)
Panama's Position
The Quest for Foreign Affairs Officers (with Francis Fielder)
The History of Sandy Hook, New Jersey
Outline of Social Sciences
Outline of Western Civilization

THOUGHTS/COMMENTS

THOUGHTS/COMMENTS